Contents

Scholastic Children's Books,
Commonwealth House, 1-19 New Oxford Street,
London WC1A 1NU, UK

A division of Scholastic Ltd
London ~ New York ~ Toronto ~ Sydney ~ Auckland
Mexico City ~ New Delhi ~ Hong Kong

Published in the UK by Scholastic Ltd, 2002

Text and illustrations copyright © Knife & Packer, 2002

ISBN 0 439 98283 9

All rights reserved
Printed by Cox & Wyman Ltd, Reading, Berks

2 4 6 8 10 9 7 5 3 1

The right of Knife & Packer to be identified as authors and illustrators of this work
has been asserted by them in accordance with the Copyright, Designs and Patents
Act, 1988.

Father Christmas unwrapped!

The world is FULL of great mysteries...

| THE LOCH NESS MONSTER | THE YETI | AND WHY DO WE HAVE BOGEYS? |

But there's one mystery that's bigger than all of these put together, a mystery so HUMUNGOUS that we, Knife and Packer, just *had* to investigate. Never mind the big beard and the jolly laugh ... **who exactly *is* Father Christmas?**

We had to do what no one has ever done before – find out where he lives and track him down... And would *you* know how to find him? It's not like he's in the phone book or anything. Fortunately we found an old map in our attic...

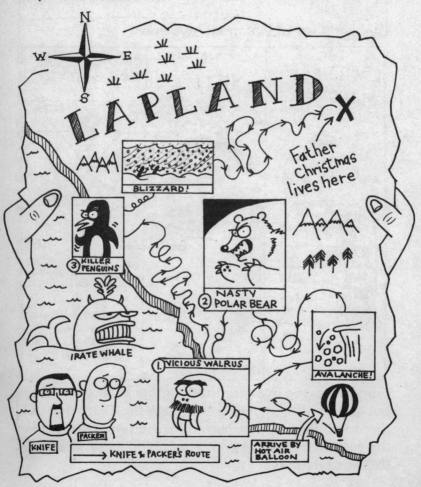

It's a miracle we made it in one piece. (The last person who tried it got eaten alive by killer penguins!)

We'd had enough, and were going to give up our quest...

Then something amazing happened. We were having a cup of tea at an Eskimo café, when we were approached by a mysterious individual...

It was RUDOLPH (you know, the reindeer with the red nose) and he'd been watching us all along! He told us to get into his car. (Remember: **you** should never get into a car with a strange reindeer. But **we** were on a mission!)

In fact he was taking us to Father Christmas – who wanted to meet us! We couldn't believe our luck!

Not only that, they wanted to help us with our book! It turns out Father Christmas is sick and tired of always being shown as a fat jolly man who says "Ho, ho, ho" all the time. He wants the world to know what being FC is *really* like...

And it's not all smiley snowmen and happy Little Helpers. Can *you* handle seeing…

If any of these knock the stuffing out of your turkey then we suggest you wrap this book up and give it to Granny...

11

But if you think you can cope, then hold on to your baubles! The information we've unearthed is guaranteed to blow your Christmas stockings RIGHT OFF...

Christmas will never be the same again as Knife and Packer bring you...

Father Christmas: the NAKED TRUTH!

Down Father Christmas's chimney

The first thing we wanted to find out from Father Christmas was where he lived. We've all seen the pictures on Christmas cards...

But the NAKED TRUTH is, it's nothing like that! (The house on the Christmas card burned down when FC accidentally left a pepperoni pizza in the oven all night...)

In fact, Father Christmas has lived in lots of different places...

But after all these disasters Father Christmas finally found somewhere he really liked. And if you can keep a secret then the NAKED TRUTH will make your tinsel tingle...

Because FC lives...

ATTIC: FULL OF OLD CHRISTMAS STUFF — MOTH-EATEN UNIFORMS, BALD CHRISTMAS TREES, ANCIENT WRAPPING PAPER COLLECTION, DENTED BAUBLES

baubles

INDUSTRIAL-SIZED HAIR DRIER FOR BEARD, MOUSTACHE AND COAT

ANTLER BRUSHES FOR THE WELL-GROOMED REINDEER

RUDI'S STABLE

DE LUXE POWER FLUSH LAVATORY FOR REINDEER DROPPINGS

CARROT-O-MATIC (CAN PEEL AND PROCESS 1,000 CARROTS A MINUTE)

mmm COMFY

FC'S ARMCHAIR

Rudi's Basket

PIZZA OVEN FOR FC'S FAVOURITE SNACK

The amazing thing is that no one in the street has any idea who their famous neighbours are. FC and Rudi will go to any lengths to avoid being pestered for early Christmas presents and autographs...

But what about living with a reindeer?

Well, there are good bits...

And bad bits…

But at least when the bad bits get seriously bad, FC can always escape to his bedroom...

Even if Rudi never stops nagging him to tidy it up!

So the NAKED TRUTH is that, at home, FC's life isn't that different from yours (except for the living-with-a-reindeer bit!). It's only when he leaves the house and puts on *that* uniform that he really becomes Father Christmas...

Suits you, Santa!

Lots of jobs have uniforms...

IT MAKES ME FEEL MILITARY!

IT MAKES ME FEEL SCHOOL DINNERLY!

IT MAKES ME FEEL CHRISTMASSY!

So what makes Father Christmas's so special? We wanted to get up close and personal, from the top of his hat to the tip of his shiny boots...

It turns out Father Christmas's uniform hasn't always been red and fluffy. The NAKED TRUTH is, it's taken a long, long time to get today's snazzy look. So here's a

'Short History of Embarrassing Uniforms'.

How ridiculous do *they* look? But today's outfit is not only a lot more stylish, it's actually much *more* than just a uniform... And for the first time EVER, FC agreed to let us have a close look at...

TECHNO - SUIT

JACKET

BEARD GROOMING KIT: KEEPS FC LOOKING SHARP AT **ALL** TIMES

DISGUISE: JUST IN CASE FC BUMPS INTO YOU!!!

TV SO HE CAN KEEP TRACK OF UP-TO-DATE WEATHER REPORTS

WATCHES SHOWING DIFFERENT TIME ZONES

REINFORCED POCKET TO CARRY CARROT SNACKS FOR RUDI

INSTANT CHRISTMAS TREE: JUST ADD WATER AND STAND BACK!

'CHIMNEYS OF THE WORLD': ESSENTIAL GUIDE (FC's NEVER WITHOUT A COPY)

26

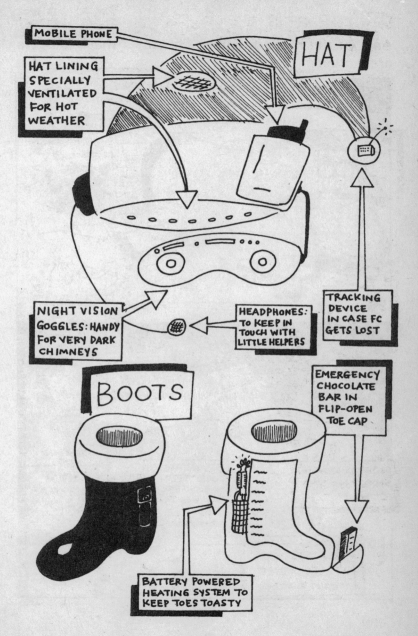

MOBILE PHONE

HAT

HAT LINING SPECIALLY VENTILATED FOR HOT WEATHER

NIGHT VISION GOGGLES: HANDY FOR VERY DARK CHIMNEYS

HEADPHONES: TO KEEP IN TOUCH WITH LITTLE HELPERS

TRACKING DEVICE IN CASE FC GETS LOST

BOOTS

EMERGENCY CHOCOLATE BAR IN FLIP-OPEN TOE CAP

BATTERY POWERED HEATING SYSTEM TO KEEP TOES TOASTY

And for the modern Father Christmas these gadgets are a must!

Although the Techno-suit isn't always used strictly for business...

But Father Christmas has another high-tech secret, one he doesn't want the world to know about. Rudolph snuck us into FC's room and opened his bottom drawer...

to reveal his...

SILLY

BIRTHDAY PANTS: WORN ONLY ON FC's BIRTHDAY: COMPLETE WITH BALLOONS!

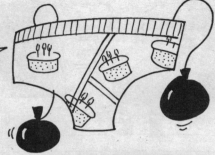

LUCKY FOOTBALL PANTS: WORN TO ALL SNOWMAN UNITED GAMES: COMPLETE WITH WHISTLE

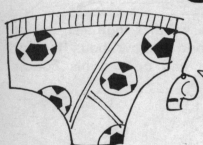

EASTER PANTS: WORN ON EASTER DAY FOR EGG-HUNTING. WITH EGG POUCH HIDING PLACE

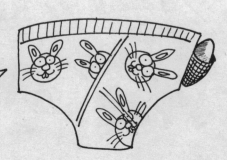

PANTS

PIZZA PANTS:
WITH SPECIAL PIZZA POCKET TO STORE A SNACK

WE THREE KINGS

MUSICAL PANTS:
PLAY FC'S FAVOURITE CHRISTMAS CAROLS WHEN HE'S BORED

SILENT NIGHT

CHRISTMAS PANTS:
WITH AN EMERGENCY MAP OF THE WORLD IN CASE HE GETS LOST DELIVERING PRESENTS (AUSTRALIA & NEW ZEALAND ON BACK)

Wow! Space-age pants *and* a high-tech uniform.
There's only one slight drawback...

Have sleigh, will travel

So how does FC get around? Father Christmas has had many sleighs over the years. You'll probably recognize this one: it's beautifully hand-carved and is pulled by reindeer, with room for one Santa and about half a dozen presents.

Delivering presents in *that* sleigh was like trying to empty the ocean with a teacup! FC realized he needed a new model a while ago. So he and Rudi did some experimenting. FC was a bit embarrassed, but he did let us have a peek at what they came up with...

These were such catastrophes that FC even considered doing away with a sleigh altogether...

Even though a bicycle and skateboard were keeping FC fit, there was a real risk that Christmas wasn't going to happen at all! It was time for something radical... FC employed a team of top boffins to come up with the sleigh of the future – jam-packed with gadgets and gizmos...

And, after working round the clock, day in, day out, they finally made the breakthrough...

Yes, for the first time ever we can exclusively unveil...

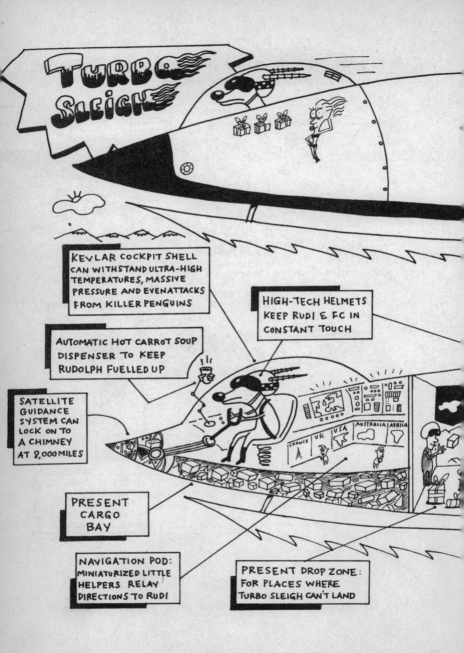

TURBO SLEIGH

KEVLAR COCKPIT SHELL CAN WITHSTAND ULTRA-HIGH TEMPERATURES, MASSIVE PRESSURE AND EVEN ATTACKS FROM KILLER PENGUINS

HIGH-TECH HELMETS KEEP RUDI & FC IN CONSTANT TOUCH

AUTOMATIC HOT CARROT SOUP DISPENSER TO KEEP RUDOLPH FUELLED UP

SATELLITE GUIDANCE SYSTEM CAN LOCK ON TO A CHIMNEY AT 8,000 MILES

PRESENT CARGO BAY

NAVIGATION POD: MINIATURIZED LITTLE HELPERS RELAY DIRECTIONS TO RUDI

PRESENT DROP ZONE: FOR PLACES WHERE TURBO SLEIGH CAN'T LAND

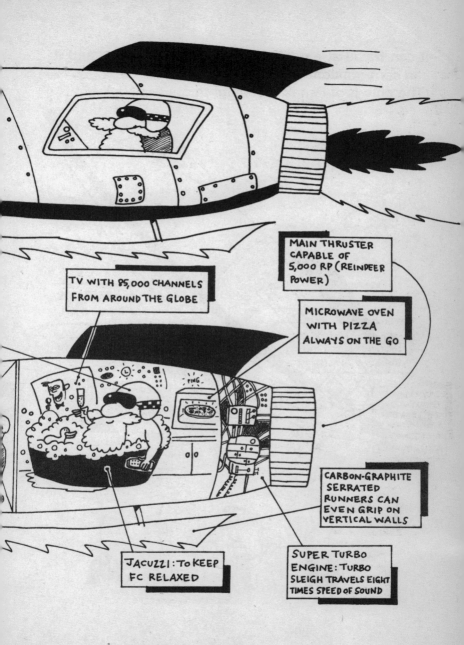

MAIN THRUSTER CAPABLE OF 5,000 RP (REINDEER POWER)

TV WITH 85,000 CHANNELS FROM AROUND THE GLOBE

MICROWAVE OVEN WITH PIZZA ALWAYS ON THE GO

CARBON-GRAPHITE SERRATED RUNNERS CAN EVEN GRIP ON VERTICAL WALLS

JACUZZI: TO KEEP FC RELAXED

SUPER TURBO ENGINE: TURBO SLEIGH TRAVELS EIGHT TIMES SPEED OF SOUND

It can travel at eight times the speed of sound and it can carry millions of presents!
(The only problem is, it's a nightmare to park.)

You don't have to be mad to work here...

We'd seen the house, we'd seen the suit and we'd seen the sleigh. But where do all the prezzies come from? That was what we really wanted to know. Father Christmas told us that the Factory had come a long way from the days when a handful of Little Helpers would carve wooden toys...

WELL DONE, JEFFREY! THAT'S THE SECOND TOY SOLDIER YOU'VE MADE THIS WEEK!

Two Little Helpers and some woodworking skills, that was good enough for the old days ... but nowadays, well, *you* do the maths! *Number of kids that live on your street X number of streets in your town X number of towns in the world = The NAKED TRUTH. That Factory has got to be GINORMOUS...*

And we were given 'access all areas'...

44

45

FC has the best Little Helpers in the business and they work, rest and play in the factory. We took a peek at their living quarters…

We wondered whether FC had a big flashy office of his own. For the first time *ever* he agreed to show the world...

THE NERVE CENTRE

MEGALIFT: GETS FC FROM GROUND TO 500th FLOOR IN LESS TIME THAN IT TAKES HIM TO COMB HIS BEARD

VIDEOTRON: DOZENS OF SCREENS ALLOW FC TO SEE WHAT'S HAPPENING ON THE SHOP FLOOR. THEY'RE EVEN FITTED IN THE LITTLE HELPERS' LOOS!

LIFT   500th FLOOR

OOH MY FOOT!

LITTLE HELPERS ON MINI SCOOTERS RUSH FC'S ORDERS TO ALL CORNERS OF THE FACTORY: WATCH YOUR TOES!

URGENT DELIVERY FOR MR FC!

49

Wow! So now you've seen the Christmas Factory ... well, most of it. But our investigations didn't stop there. There was one place we'd heard all about that FC *absolutely refused* to let us visit. Once again, Rudi came to the rescue...

The Present Laboratory

This place is *Strictly Off Limits* except to a few of the most trusted Little Helpers. It's the place where Father Christmas invents new toys. We just HAD to have a look.

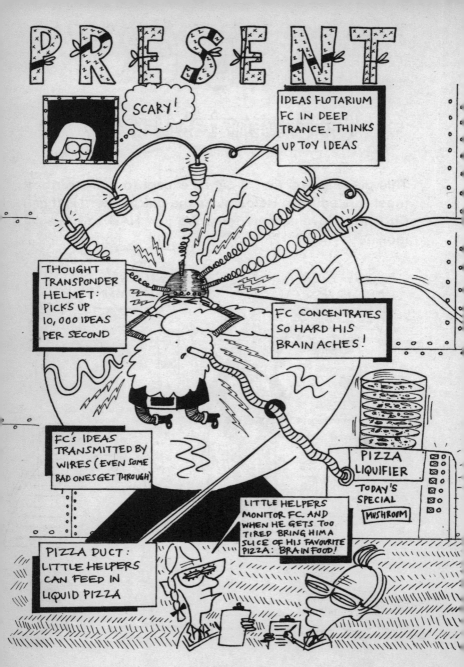

LABORATORY

DENTIST ACTION FIGURE

"I'LL BE BACK TO GIVE YOU A FILLING"

TALKS

VIBRATING DRILL

MOUTHWASH BEAKER

THOUGHT VISUALIZATION UNIT: WE SEE FC'S IDEAS ON SCREEN

LOLLIPOP-LADY DOLL

WITH PACKED LUNCH!

STOP

TALKING KIDS!

"CAN WE CROSS NOW, MISS?"

ONLY THE BEST ONES ARE PRINTED OUT

TAP TAP TAP TAP

DAD

TAP

LITTLE HELPER STORES ALL IDEAS ON DATABASE FOR FUTURE REFERENCE

Amazing! So that's where the present ideas come from! But there was more – the Present Laboratory has an Experimental Wing...

All new presents have to be rigorously tested and FC has a crack team of Toy Testers headed up by Professor Squiffy...

Every week Professor Squiffy shows FC how his inventions are coming along.

And every year there's a huge awards ceremony for the best toys invented for that Christmas ... and the winner is always...

Which is hardly surprising seeing as he's the only person competing!

And that's how toys are invented. But how does Father Christmas know what *you* would like for Christmas? Well, have you ever written to him? Rudi had one last secret to let us in on. But we had to get to the outermost limits of the Christmas Factory grounds...

Before finally reaching...

7

Father Christmas's Secret Letter Library...

So what happens to your letter when you post it to FC?

The NAKED TRUTH is: every single letter ends up in FC's Secret Letter Library. We desperately needed to have a good snoop round…

Wow! We'd never seen so many letters! How on earth could FC read *all of them*? The NAKED TRUTH is: it's all down to his 'Insecto-Spex', which give FC hundreds of eyeballs (just like a fly). He can read 10,000 letters a minute!!! Rudi gave us a demonstration...

We wanted to have a go but there wasn't time. And Rudi had something else he wanted to show us...

At the back of the library, behind a hidden panel, there was a Top-Secret File that Rudi said we *had* to have a closer look at.

These letters are *so* silly that FC doesn't want *anyone* to see them!

It was *so* embarrassing, until Rudi turned the page…

With so many ridiculous letters it's amazing anyone ever gets what they actually want! We asked Rudi what kind of letters FC liked best, and which were the most likely to get results. Was it the Wacky ones? The Musical ones? The Crazy-Shaped ones? No, the NAKED TRUTH is: it's the *Crawling* ones!!!

To help you out next Christmas, over the page is a Rudi-approved Crawling Letter that you can cut out and send to Lapland. (Have a Christmas stocking to hand, though, you might find it a queasy read!)

Dear Father Christmas

I think you're great. When I grow up I want to have a beard just like yours — because it's super!!!

GREAT BEARD!

I understand that you are a very busy man but if you could try and squeeze me in I'd be very very grateful. And I'd like a

_____

for Christmas (if you've got the time).

Lots of love _____ ♡ xxx

PS You must be awfully brainy to be FC!

YUK!

CREEPY!

WHERE'S THE BATHROOM?

Let's get ready to rumble! Christmas Eve!

The letters have been read, the presents are packed and ready to go... It's Action Stations as FC gets down to the most crucial part of his business: delivering presents... So, as you go to sleep on Christmas Eve ... what do you think FC's doing?

The NAKED TRUTH is: he's...

We can now bring you a **WORLD EXCLUSIVE** as we hitch a ride with FC!

It's a roller-coaster, seat-of-your-pants ride, as we take off aboard Turbo Sleigh for the trip of a lifetime...

And when FC gets going we can barely keep up with him.

71

But Christmas Eve isn't all about zooming around the globe, it's also about getting in and out of houses delivering the presents. FC invited us to join him for some of them. Here are his:

'Four Steps For A Smooth Delivery'

With so many houses to deliver to, all this was done in a flash! The only time FC took a breather was when he looked at the notes and goodies you left out for him. And FC scoffed the lot! We didn't get so much as a crumb!

What a trip! We were absolutely exhausted. As we left Rudi and FC to spend the last few hours of Christmas Eve together, we could only imagine what fun they were having...

Christmas Day – Phew!

It's Christmas morning and as you're sorting through your stocking, what's that in the sky?

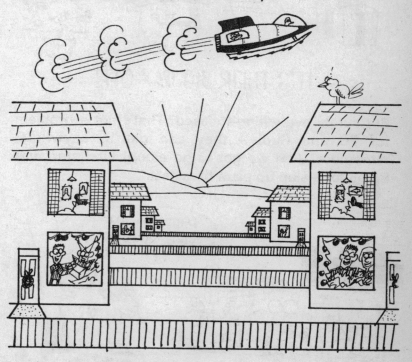

You're too busy opening presents to notice Father Christmas and Rudi, but what are they up to?

The NAKED TRUTH is: by the time Christmas Day comes, the last thing they want to see is wrapping paper or a Christmas tree...

IT'S THEIR BIG DAY OFF!

But surely everything's closed? That's not a problem for FC and Rudi – they can get in anywhere, remember? And we got to go along! First stop was Rome for a slap-up pizza breakfast.

Next, we hit the shops in New York! Think about it: Christmas day is the only time Father Christmas can go to the shops without being pestered.

But it's not just the shopping – it's also the only chance for FC to have a haircut! (In Paris – *naturellement!*)

And for Rudi to have a good 'spring clean'.

There was still plenty of time to have fun, too! We stopped in Silverstone, Hollywood *and* Australia!

What an exhausting day! We were relieved to climb into Turbo Sleigh and head back to Lapland.

Our time with Father Christmas was running out and there was one last favour we wanted to ask him. And after a lot of persuasion (and an 85-inch pepperoni pizza)

FC finally agreed.

The scoop of the Millennium!

At last, the moment you've all been waiting for: our World Exclusive interview with Father Christmas (and Rudi)...

First things first: What's the best thing about being Father Christmas?

So many things, the smart uniform, the Turbo Sleigh,

having first go on new toys...

And I get to hang out with my best mate...

We know you're best mates but is there anything about Rudi that *really* bugs you?

Only when he's moulting – the hair gets everywhere (and I'm allergic).

Great!

WHEEZE SNEEZE

I'VE HEARD OF BAD HAIR DAYS!

And, Rudi, what about FC? He's got to have some bad habits?

He never throws his old pizza boxes out!

HELP! I'M A PRISONER OF PEPPERONI!

What's the most embarrassing thing that's ever happened to you?

It has to be the time when I was delivering presents to the White House and my bottom got stuck in the chimney...

It took three FBI officers to get me out. I made them promise not to tell anyone. Now I'm in their X-files you know!

Rudi, does FC often get stuck in chimneys?

Fortunately not, but we have a device that we use in extreme situations. It's called the Mega Plunger (a bit like the one you've got in your loo, only bigger!).

So why did you settle in Lapland? It's miles from anywhere and hardly anyone lives here...

Exactly! Being Father Christmas, I couldn't live in a big city, could I? Imagine if I took the bus...

Not only that but I get on very well with reindeer and penguins...

Do *you* celebrate Christmas and if so what's the worst present anyone ever delivered to you?

Last Christmas the Little Helpers thought that Rudi needed a rest and bought me a camel called Gerald.

Unfortunately Gerald and Rudi didn't hit it off

and we had to fly him back to the desert...

So Rudi never did get a break? It must be exhausting for you, too. Have you ever had a Christmas off?

Nearly. There was one year when I had terrible flu and the doctor ordered me to stay in bed.

My cousin Miguel from Panama was drafted in...

What happened?

He got the presents mixed up and the date confused – he delivered a week early!!! It was a complete disaster – the Queen woke up one morning to find her bed covered in Guatamalan Tree Frogs (which should have been delivered to an Indian chief in the Amazon jungle).

So was Christmas cancelled?

Oh no! Totally against doctors' orders, I had to drag myself out of bed to get the job done!

ONLY 150,000 TO GO!

SNIFFLE
SNUFFLE
SNIFFLE

That sounds terrible! You must get really stressed – how do you relax?

I collect Christmas cards. It's hilarious! The pictures of Father Christmas look nothing like me!

Rudi and I also support Snowman United and try to catch as many games as we can. But they're not doing very well this season.

UNLESS THEY CAN SCORE 6 GOALS IN THE LAST MINUTE, SNOWMAN UNITED ARE GOING DOWN!

You seem to be pizza potty. What's that all about?

Every Christmas Eve people leave out mince pies, mince pies, mince pies, I'm sick of Christmas food! Give me pizza any day!

HEY, FC! I'VE GOT A NEW PIZZA FOR YOU — MINCE PIE TOPPING!

Rudi, you're a bit of a whizz in the kitchen. What's your favourite meal?

GRADE A CARROTS

FOR STARTERS, CARROT COCKTAIL FOLLOWED BY ROAST CARROTS WITH CARROT GRAVY. AND CARROT TRIFLE FOR PUD!

Have you always had *that* beard?

No, I've tried all kinds of beards but I always seem to end up looking silly.

GENIE

THREE MUSKETEERS

VIKING

Once I even shaved it off but it gave Rudi the fright of his life!

TIME TO GO!

We still had lots of questions to ask but Rudi reminded Father Christmas that they had to start getting ready for *next* Christmas.

Before we knew it we were being blindfolded...

And led to the Turbo Sleigh. Soon we were zooming back over the factory...

MIND THE CHIMNEYS, RUDI!

Past the Eskimo café...

ICE LOLLIES HALF PRICE

COME BACK! YOU NEVER PAID US FOR THOSE TEAS

Past the killer penguins...

WE'LL GET YOU NEXT TIME!!